ACKNOWLEDGEMENTS:

Special thanks to Mike Wood, Paul Sudbury,
Mary Killingworth, Mark Peacock, Joanne Meeks,
all at Generation Associates, all keen rugby fans across
the country - and the man who made it all possible -
Tim Forrester.

A special thanks to Adrian Murrell
and all the lads at Allsport.

Dedicated to Chinnor RFC

To play with style and provide an atmosphere of
warmth and camaraderie tinged with a sizeable slice of ambition.

John Brooks, Tim Wright, James Davies, John Vaughan,
James Walkinshaw, John Sellars, Patric Jobson, Gary Pudwell,
Richard John, Simon Matthews, Gary Porter, Warren Bright,
John Brown, Stuart Tinegate, Michael Cook, Matthew Cooke,
Paul Fincken, Richard Cartwright, Andrew Milburn.
Team Manager - Glyn Davies
Coach - Lyn Evans
Ever Presents - Fred Read, Ally Davies

"Rugby may be entering a brave new professional and commercial age but for me its heart and soul will always be face down in the mud at the bottom of a ruck on a cold, wet weekend in February.

This book of jokes, quotes and stories celebrates 'real' rugby at its grubby, gritty best and is dedicated to all the Saturday afternoon heroes - 'fat boys' or 'girls' - whose only taste of glory is served by the barman after yet another 50 point drubbing! Enjoy!"

Dean Richards

Tongan team express their opinion of a female supporter walking past.

6

7

LESSON LEARNED

HAWICK AND SCOTLAND PROP HUGH MCLEOD found a young opponent attempting to tarnish his huge reputation as one of Scotland's finest. The young upstart prop opposite McLeod said loudly: "I wonder what lesson the great Mr McLeod has for us today?" McLeod, noting the sarcasm, took the opportunity to rest his foot on the upstart's hand as he caught his balance in a scrum. As McLeod added weight to his step on the unfortunate's hand, he whispered in his ear: "Here endeth the first lesson, Sonny."

NO JOB SECURITY

THE ENGLAND SIDE OF THE MID-1980s was hardly a stable one. Between January 1984 and January 1985, first caps were awarded to no fewer than 23 players.

ON A HIDING

NORWICH entered the record books when they notched up a 177-3 Norfolk Cup quarter final win over minnows Eccles & Attleborough. It was the biggest score ever in a senior game between two English clubs. Eccles captain David Goreham said afterwards: "Our target was to keep the score below three figures but whatever happened we did not want to forego the game as some clubs have done in similar circumstances. We played for the sake of rugby. We expected a hiding, although not that much of one."

"You can't go from amateur to professionalism overnight. If we go too far too soon and realise we have made a mistake, then there is no way we wind back the clock."
SERGE BLANCO

"He is the sort of player whose brain doesn't always know where his legs are carrying him."
NICK FARR JONES ON CAMPO

OH, CALCUTTA

THE 1988 CALCUTTA CUP MATCH between Scotland and England had continued to be played long after the final whistle. The handsome old trophy, made from Indian rupees, was taken out into Edinburgh, by among others, Scotland's John Jeffreys and England's Dean Richards. An impromptu game ensued, with the Cup as the ball. It suffered a bit of damage along the way, and was informally referred to as the Calcutta Plate until it was repaired.

BAA-BAAS IN FLIGHT

RUGBY can lay claim to quite possibly the most memorable piece of sporting commentary after Kenneth Wolstenholme's World Cup Final 1966 "They think it's all over - it is now."

The occasion was the Barbarians against New Zealand at Cardiff 1973 and a try that will live in memories of all those who saw it at the game and on TV forever.

As the Baa-Baas swept from one end of the pitch to the other, started by Phil Bennett's jinking run out of defence, TV commentator Cliff Morgan almost ran out of breath:

"This is great stuff. Phil Bennett covering, chased by Alistair Scown. Brilliant; John Williams, Bryan Williams... Pullin... John Dawes, great dummy... David, Tom David; the halfway line... brilliant by Quinnell... this is Gareth Edwards... a dramatic start. **What a score!**"

Gareth Edwards said of the try: "The more I watch the try on video, the more I wonder how an earth we scored. It was an impossible try."

COLD CAMPESE

WILL CARLING once suggested that England would never pick David Campese if he were eligible to don the English colours, because the game Campo played was "too risky." The Australian superstar replied that he "would never play for that conservative mob, anyway. The only thing you're ever likely to get on the end of an English backline is chilblains."

"Andy Gomarsall, full of zap and energy early on, became so ponderous at scrum half that he made John Major's deliberations over the General Election date look positively impetuous."

CHRIS HEWETT,
THE INDEPENDENT, 1997

'**Make that two coffins.**'

CAUGHT BEHIND THE LINES

THE ENGLAND V FRANCE Five Nations clash in 1985 should have been won by France but for an amazing piece of covering by England scrum half Nigel Melville. In the first half, French winger Patrick Esteve broke through and crossed the try line, but as he made to run behind the posts, the winger was caught by Melville, who managed to slap the ball out of Esteve's hands. The match finished in a draw.

LET THERE BE LIGHT

THE HARPER ADAMS Agricultural College rugby club fancied a few midweek evening games, but they needed floodlights. The solution? Drink like mad and use the profits from the student union bar, which totalled £14,000. They now have lights.

> **"So the rolling stock has been joined by rolling laughter and revelry in the Chunnel."**
>
> TONY UNDERWOOD IN THE INDEPENDENT AFTER FRANCE BEAT ENGLAND AT TWICKENHAM IN 1997.

BLACK FROM WHITE

KENYA changed from white to black shirts in 1935. At a fixture in Entebbe, both sides turned up wearing white - Kenya died theirs black thanks to a spectator's handy provision of some dye, and have worn black shirts ever since.

THE DRYING GAME 1

THE THIRD TEST between New Zealand and the British Lions in 1983 was played in such appalling conditions that prior to kick-off, helicopters were used to dry the pitch.

THE DRYING GAME 2

THE WELSH RUGBY AUTHORITIES found a successful ploy for thawing pitches when they were too frozen to play on. Prior to internationals in both 1893 and 1956, they burned tons of coal (18 in 1893) to thaw out the pitch sufficiently. In 1963 the French decided to thaw their pitch prior to a game against Scotland by simply setting fire to all the straw that had been strewn to protect the grass from the pitch.

**"Irish Drowning,
Not Swimming"**
INDEPENDENT HEADLINE
AFTER IRELAND LOSE
TO SCOTLAND IN 1997

'Please let us out Mister.
We didn't steal anything.'

Campo Loves England

Australia's David Campese was never one to mince words about playing England. On one occasion he boasted: "The convicts will smash the toffs."

French Farce

The 1992 France v England match contained moments of farce and theatre. The normally fluent French backs Jean Luc Sadourny and Alain Penaud managed to collide mid-move. England scored from the loose ball. And then French forwards Vincent Moscato and Gregoire Lascube were sent off for violent play.

Below Zero

Canterbury Exiles were deducted 30 points for fielding an ineligible player on three occasions. It meant that the Exiles had no mathematical chance of ending the season with a points total of better than -18.

40-Yard Dash

Les Cusworth had the honour of scoring the winning try for the Barbarians in the 1981 Hong Kong 7s, recalling: "I remember receiving the ball about 40 yards out, spotting a chink in the Wallabies defence and waddling through."

Not So Supreme

The 1995 Rugby League World Cup was officially opened by singer Diana Ross. She had also opened the 1994 football World Cup in the USA, where she suffered the embarrassment of missing the entire goal from the penalty spot when asked to hit the net to open the tournament. Fortunately, the Rugby League organisers wisely desisted from asking Ms Ross to have a go with the oval ball.

Some Traffic Jam

Travelling by boat to play Denmark in an international, the Swedish team found themselves stuck in an ice flow, from which there was no escape for eight days.

Catching The Cap

New Zealand's Jimmy Duncan always played wearing a tweed cap - primarily to cover his baldness, but it came in useful in open play, too. Once, he sold a dummy to the Aucklund defence by throwing his cap to the man outside and turning inside himself with the ball. The wrong footed defence turned to see Duncan cross the line to score.

Rugby For All

"Old and infirm welcome!" The Guilden Morden Pub Sevens opens its doors to everyone with its invite .

Throwing The Game

The 1963 match between Scotland and Wales featured 111 lineouts.

The Sound Of No Music

The only time when the National Anthems of the two teams haven't been played at Twickenham was in 1964 prior to a game between England and New Zealand. Both teams were recalled to their changing rooms before the match kicked off, but the band followed them off the pitch too. The misunderstanding meant no anthems.

> **"We must never forget how well we did in the World Cup - throughout the tournament I saw people in the stands with tears rolling down their cheeks. I saw grown men and women cry out of sheer pride. We must never forget how together we were as a nation on the day the Springboks won."**
> **Francois Pienaar**

‘ **Ooh,**
my little heart
goes pit-a-pat. ’

‘ Don't tell your Mam,
see, but we're in the
wrong rugby book. ’

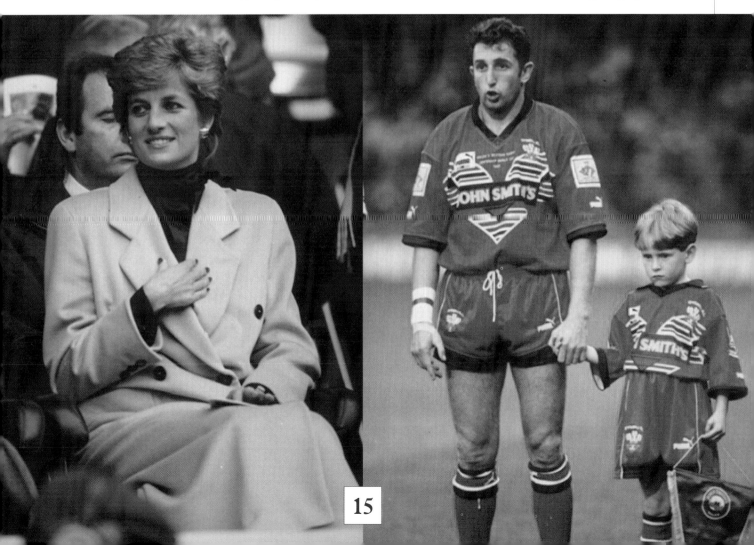

15

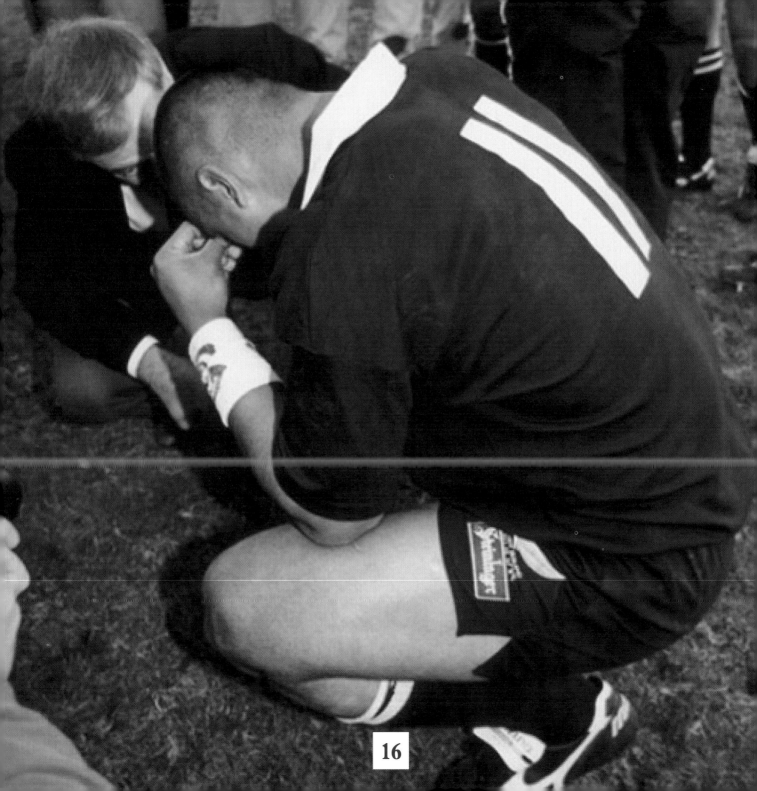

PLAYING BOTH SIDES

FRENCH CAPTAIN ABDELATIF BENAZZI actually played against France in a rugby international, a World Cup qualifying match. Bennazzi was representing his home country of Morocco. Prior to his success at rugby, Benazzi also won the Moroccan Junior Championships for shot-put and discus.

> **"Amateurism. Like scrum caps, leather studs and dubbin, it has long since disappeared from the game's landscape."**
> ROB ANDREW ON PROFESSIONALISM

> **"David Campese likes to play his rugby on the high wire - without a safety net."**
> GORDON BRAY

THE NAME GAME

CALL IT A COINCIDENCE, but England wing forward Richard Hill, who made his debut in 1996, went to the same school as a former England stalwart at scrum half, who's name was... Richard Hill.

ONE ANDY IRVINE...

SCOTTISH FULL BACK ANDY IRVINE was held in such high regard around the world that during a 1981 tour of New Zealand, an advertisement in the national press heralded the final test with a picture of All Black captain Graham Mourie stood next to Irvine. The caption under Mourie simply stated that it was his last appearance of 1981, whereas under Irvine it said "This is possibly your last chance to see this legend."

> **"In the mid eighties, selection for England was the modern equivalent of being named as accredited food taster for Attila the Hun."**
> ROB ANDREW "A GAME AND A HALF"

ARNIE'S HOUR

ARNOLD ALCOCK, an average member of the Guy's Hospital team, received a call-up to play for England against the South African tourists in 1906. Although Alcock was flabbergasted to be called into international duty, he duly turned up for the match, only then to find that the selection letter should have gone to Andrew Slocock of Blackheath. Slocock could not be located in time, so Alcock played his first, and last, international in a 3-3 draw.

> **I'll be all right in a minute; I've got Tony Underwood in my eye.**

TUCK IT!

THE MATCH PROGRAMME for the 1980 clash between France and Ireland caused some merriment among the Irish contingent, when it was discovered that the surname of loose forward Colin Tucker had been misspelt to begin with an "F".

ROB'S MONICKER

ROB ANDREW burst on to the national sporting scene at the age of 22 backed with a host of experience at the top level. He left Cambridge having won five blues, two at cricket, three at rugby, and had captained the University cricket side against the touring Australians. Small wonder, then, that the press awarded him the nickname "Golden Bollocks".

MICK GETS MUNCHING

FEW WILL FORGET one particular moment of the 1991 World Cup quarter final between England and France. It was a turning point in the game when England flanker Mick Skinner hit France's Marc Cecillon with such an almighty tackle he sent him backwards several yards and at the same time broke the French spirit. The tackle was labelled a "crushing demolition." Skinner's nickname is The Munch.

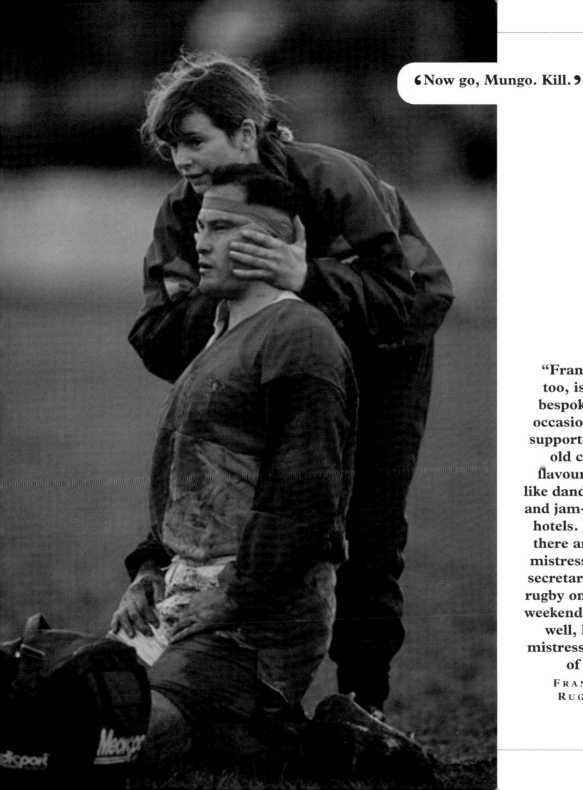

‘Now go, Mungo. Kill.’

"France to Dublin, too, is invariably a bespoke and one-off occasion. The French supporters revel in the old city's unique flavours. They dress like dandies for the trip, and jam-pack the 5-star hotels. I'm convinced there are more Gallic mistresses and bosses' secretaries over for the rugby on this particular weekend than there are, well, home-grown mistresses in the whole of Ireland."

FRANK KEATING
RUGBY WORLD

21

CHEEK FOR JOWLS

TONY O'REILLY, the legendary Irish back, played his last international against England in 1971. He was by then aged 34. Irish skipper that year was Willie John McBride, who took O'Reilly aside to issue him with some match instructions. He said: "Tony, you won't mind me saying to your face that you are no longer in your prime. The tactic I suggest you adopt is shake your jowls at your opposite number."

WURZEL CARLING

WILL CARLING'S punishment for not performing up to scratch in an England training session was to sit at lunch with a snooker cue inserted through his jacket sleeves. Carling resembled a scarecrow, and the rest of the team enjoyed watching him try to eat his soup.

I hate waiting for the headmaster.

‘And then she said she
was leaving me.’

RIGHT, LEFT

TOMMY GRAY of Scotland and Northampton used to encourage the rumour that because of a war injury he could only jink to the right. In emergencies he would leave opponents grasping air by jinking to the left instead.

BILLY THE FISH

A 1982 SCOTLAND TOUR OF AUSTRALIA nearly saw the end of Bill Cuthbertson, who got into difficulties while swimming at Surfers' Paradise. It took three players to drag him out, coughing and spluttering. He was promptly nicknamed Jacques Cousteau.

"The main difference
between playing League
and Union is that now I
get my hangovers on
Monday instead of
Sunday."
TOM DAVID

Listen To Your Dad

GARETH EDWARDS has always been a keen angler, so much so that his father once ticked him off, saying: "You'd score a lot more tries for Wales if it wasn't for those rusty kneecaps of yours from all that fishing."

"We French score tries because we cannot kick penalties."
JEAN PIERRE RIVES

"To enjoy sevens one must be either dedicated or supremely fit. Most rugby players are neither, so the sevens loom as the only cloud on a perfect season."
MICHAEL GREEN
EVEN COARSER RUGBY

Big Oli

OLIVIER MERLE, French lock forward, was christened with a nickname appropriate to his build. The former lumberjack answered to the name Massif Central, after the French mountain range. Bill Beaumont said of the 20-stone Merle: "You'd need a fork lift truck to lift him in the lineout."

A Note From His Mum

FORMER Scotland captain David Sole was due to stand in front of a disciplinary committee in 1995, but was unable to attend the hearing as he had to baby sit.

Double Barrelled Dummy

WHEN ENGLAND'S PHIL HORROCKS-TAYLOR threw Irish fly half Mick English a dummy and run in to score in the 1971 international at Twickenham, English's team-mate Tony O'Reilly commented: "Horrocks went this way, Taylor went that way, and poor old Mick was left holding the hyphen."

"The tackling part was never a problem for me. I like tackling. Putting in a good tackle is nearly as good as scoring."
CHRIS SHEASBY

"Rugby is not greedy. It is simply that the RFU, charged only with the task of being ready for lift off of the professional season, has been caught utterly unprepared, even with years of notice. Resignations to date? None."
STEPHEN JONES

Nobody's Perfect

ROB ANDREW may lay claim to being the best fly half England ever produced, but he still had a few off days. For example, when Nottingham played London Welsh in a John Player Cup game in 1985, Andrew managed to miss nine out of ten kicks at goal. Nottingham went down 12-11.

Bare Footin'

HARRY GARNETT OF BRADFORD, did not wear boots or socks throughout his entire career, preferring to play in his bare feet. This even included during his one England cap, against Scotland in 1877.

ONE EYED JOCK

SCOTTISH international Jock Wemyss lost an eye during the World War One, but still added five more caps to his collection when he returned from the fighting.

CRAZY DRIVER

DURING the 1993 British Lions tour of New Zealand, Ireland's Mick Galwey managed the distinction of being banned from the nation's entire complement of go-karting tracks because of his rather reckless driving technique.

❛Yup. The English fullback is showing signs of being very frightened.❜

‘We know you respect the All Blacks, but this is ridiculous.’

Sssh. Ssstoppit. Not anuzer drop until the game is over.

MEATY, BEATY, BIG AND BOUNCY

THE 19-STONE JONAH LOMU was even big at birth, he weighed 11 pounds.

I HEARD THAT

IRISH HOOKER KEITH WOOD joined Harlequins and ran into a language problem: "I don't understand everything Laurent (Benezech) is saying but it's easier than Jason's cockney language. Then we have the Llewellyn brothers with their sing song Welsh and as for Mick Watson, well, I can't understand a word."

HAT'S ON

FRENCH THREE-QUARTER ANDREA BEHOTEGUY always wore a beret when he played.

"We want players with a totally singleminded determination and a desire to walk on broken glass if that's what it takes to win the Test series. If you are not certain, don't go."
MANAGER FRAN COTTON ON BRITISH LIONS 1997

I can see its head
coming out!
It's a boy.

28

"We had played three warm-up matches, we had devoted every waking hour to thinking about it but, when the time came, we froze. Simple as that. In golfing parlance, we got the yips."

ROB ANDREW ON ENGLAND'S 1991 WORLD CUP AGAINST THE ALL BLACKS

Ref...
he's calling me
names.

NO KIDDING

BASIL MACLEAN, who played for Ireland 11 times between 1905 and 1907, always wore white kid gloves when playing.

WHAT'S IN A NAME?

NICKNAME: All Black ST Reid preferred that people call him by shortened version of his Christian name, hence "Tori". Hardly surprising really, as his first name was actually Sanitorium.

ANDREW'S FIRST

ROB ANDREW made his international debut against Romania in January 1985, and scored his first points for his country in just 47 seconds, dropping a goal.

I'M OFF

WESTERN SAMOAN international Saini Lemamea announced his retirement in a curious manner, he went walkabout in the outback and never returned.

FAMOUS NAMES

BILL CLINTON was a rugby player in his days at Oxford, turning out in the second row. Idi Amin, the former leader of Uganda, was also a keen player, and in fact was an official reserve for a 1959 game between East Africa and the British Lions.

SUPERSTITIOUS

MOST SPORTSMEN have superstitions, and legendary Scottish hooker Colin Deans was no exception. He made his home debut for Hawick against Ballymena, a game Hawick won. After that game Deans tried as hard as he could to ensure he used the same peg in the changing room for each home match he played.

**Nah, nothing special.
Tuesday night her
mother come round and
we had a curry.
What did you get up to ?**

What do you mean it ended five minutes ago?

32

THE BRAIN GAME

ENGLAND HOOKER MARK REGAN summed up the qualities required to play in the front row: "You need a mental toughness. And probably don't need to be too bright."

GERALD

WELSH WINGER GERALD DAVIES inspired awe among all rugby fans, and in a few of his opponents, too. England winger David Duckham said of the fleet-footed Davies: "You know exactly what he is going to do. He's going to come off his right foot at great speed. You also know that there isn't a blind thing you can do about it."

SPELL CHECK

GARETH EDWARDS threw his forwards into confusion during a practice session before a Five Nations match. Welsh coach John Dawes was implementing a system of codewords for back row moves, to be called by scrum half Edwards. Words starting with "P" meant a break to the left, "S" to the right. At the first scrum, Edwards put the ball in and called "Psychology."

BIG WADE

NO-ONE CAN DISPUTE Roger Uttley's qualities as player and coach. But his motivational abilities were basic, as his speech to the British Lions pack prior to the second Test against Australia in 1989 showed. In the style of the captains of golf's Ryder Cup matches between USA and Europe, Uttley went through the forwards one by one to gee them up: "David Sole, the most mobile prop in the world; Brian Moore, the most competitive hooker in the world; Paul Ackford the best front jumper in the world..." and so on, until Uttley came to Wade Dooley: "And Dooley - you're replacing Bob Norster, the best line out jumper in the world, the best lock forward in the world - you're in the side because you're big."

"He's a freak and the sooner he goes away the better."
WILL CARLING
ON LOMU

"I was fortunate because, when I joined Leicester in 1982, there were still players who liked to go out for a beer, even on the Thursday and Friday night before a game. Now the game has become more serious and players do not drink from Saturday to Saturday. They are the orange juice brigade. It has all changed since my first international season; the night before playing France in Paris, Steve Brain and I had a few pints. We wouldn't do that now."
DEAN RICHARDS ON THE MODERN GAME.

WHO NEEDS BACKS?

ROBERT THOMPSON of Western Australia holds the distinction of being a goal kicking hooker. The talented front row player took up kicking to strengthen his leg after injury, and obviously took a shine to it.

EYE FOR AN EYE

JOCK WEMYSS lost an eye during World War 1 but still managed to add to his number of international caps for Scotland after the war. In one match against France he heard that the French forward Lubin-Lebrere also had only one eye, so they arranged to mark each other, which led to a certain amount of groping for the ball in the line-outs. The referee had a mind to penalise them at one stage, but the Scottish captain, Charlie Usher pleaded: "Leave them alone, ref, they're both half blind!"

'Please, Lord, please don't let me catch it.'

"David Campese plays in two cities which possess the most beautiful opera houses in the world - Sydney and Milan. And in the opera of rugby, Campese is the absolute star, a bounding Pavarotti."

L'EQUIPE

‘ Put that away! ’

But mister you can have the ball. We don't want to tackle you.

KISS THIS

FRENCH STAND OFF MARTINE showed remarkable coolness and not a little Gallic flair when, during a test match against South Africa in 1958, he received a pass, and despite the fact the Springbok loose forwards were bearing down on him, took the time to kiss the ball before landing a 40-yard drop goal to clinch a rare victory on South African soil.

I.. am.. too.. old..
for.. all.. this...

PROP KICKER

AARON GEFFIN laid claim to being one of rugby's best place kickers during the 1950s, which is not the accolade you usually find bestowed on a prop forward. The story goes that Geffin spent his time in a Prisoner of War camp during World War II practising his kicking with a rugby ball smuggled into the camp.

HAVE YOU GOT YOUR FEET?

OBSERVER journalist and author of Coarse Rugby Michael Green noted that the Rugby Football Union's early coaching manuals tended to state the blinding obvious. The qualities required for a full back were, for example: "hands, position, tackle, speed, two feet."

THE GREAT BARRY JOHN

PEOPLE used to say of the brilliant Welsh fly half Barry John that he never seemed to leave a room by the door, he just drifted through the wall.

'Pretty funny ya?
On the wing, Ha ha ha.'

THE FULL BACK

"THERE ARE MANY JOBS TO BE AVOIDED IN COARSE RUGBY," wrote Michael Green in Even Coarser Rugby. "Among those that leap to mind, full back stands out in particular. He watches with growing apprehension the feeble efforts of his three quarters to tackle, the complete absence of cover, and the certain knowledge that as soon as by some miracle the opposition can give and take four passes in succession without dropping the ball, he will be faced by three opponents with not a friend in sight. Not only that, but everyone will blame him as they line up for the conversion kick."

"In 1823, William Webb Ellis first picked up the ball in his arms and ran with it. And for the next 156 years forwards have been trying to work out why."

SIR TASKER WATKINS

"The backs preen
themselves and the
forwards drink."
DEAN RICHARDS

Cover tackle.

Fishing tackle.

Wedding tackle.

ERIKA'S ASSETS

ONE OF TWICKENHAM'S FINEST SIGHTS was probably Erika Roe, who famously showed her well endowed chest to the world during the 1982 season. When she ran on to the pitch, England scrum half Steve Smith called over to captain Bill Beaumont: "Bill, there's a bird just run on with your bum on her chest."

GRANNY BASHER

CAPTAIN of the French touring side to New Zealand in 1961, Michel Crauste, found himself attacked by a member of the crowd during a match against South Canterbury. Crauste turned to exact revenge on his assailant only to find the person hitting him around the back and head was a woman, roughly in her 60s.

CAN WE HAVE OUR BALL BACK, PLEASE?

THE WEST WALES Challenge Cup Final in 1877, a match between mighty rivals Cardiff and Llanelli, had to be abandoned due to a spectator stealing the ball.

CARD GAME

RUGBY WORLD magazine gave the fans the chance to express their views to the referee during the 1997 England v France game at Twickenham. Included in the souvenir give-away handed out by Rugby World to fans before the match was a yellow card, designed to be waved at the ref whenever there was foul play. The RFU was not amused.

IN CELEBRATION

WILLIE JOHN McBRIDE found that the match against Wales in 1975, in the centenary year for Irish rugby, was not one that followed the theme of celebration: "We got absolutely thrashed. Then afterwards two guys came towards me with green and white scarves - they had obviously had a hell of a day. One of them recognised me and said 'I know this is the centenary of the IRFU, but there's no need to play like one of the founder members."

"No-one has ever suggested that Old Rubber Duckians should start paying their guys for playing."
BRIAN MOORE

An All Black mother prepares to give birth.

DROPPING GOALS

THE RIGHT QUALIFICATIONS

FORMER SCOTTISH INTERNATIONAL and now rugby pundit Ian Robertson experienced an interesting entrance exam for Cambridge University. The professor was sports mad, and when Robertson entered the room, the professor threw a rugby ball to him. Robertson not only caught the ball, but then drop kicked it into a waste bin, thus sealing his entrance into the prestigious university.

JONES DROPS ONE

ROBERT JONES, another in a long line of brilliant Wales scrum halves, would rather forget a drop goal attempt he made against Ireland in a Five Nations clash. Jones stubbed the ground with his foot and managed to send the ball no more than three yards. What's more, the Irish collected the ball, ran up field and scored.

AGAINST ORDERS

IN THE DAYS when a drop goal was worth four points, Cliff Morgan, who later became a Welsh legend in the no. 10 shirt, was always reluctant to take a pot, remembering the words of his schoolmaster Ned Gribble - "Never drop a goal." When he did, securing a 4-3 win for his school, Gribble tore a strip off the young Morgan for spurning the chance of a try, and as punishment did not pick Morgan for the next two games.

MOVING TARGET

WHEN A GUST OF WIND blew the posts over just as Ian Robertson was lining up a drop goal attempt for Public School Wanderers, the fly half kept his cool and duly slotted the ball between the fallen posts to register three points.

"Being dropped by England and Take That splitting up on the same day is enough to finish anyone off."
MARTIN BAYFIELD

MAKING A POINT

ROB ANDREW aided his progress into the Cambridge University side by actually playing against them for a side in Sunderland. Two 40 yard drop goals did his cause no harm at all.

A MAN OF MANY TALENTS

MIGHTY ALL BLACK back row forward Zinzan Brooke is one the game's most competitive players, and he's pretty talented with it, too. One of his claims to fame is that he has an international drop goal to his credit, and not just any drop goal, either. Brooke potted a 45-yard effort in the 1995 World Cup semi-final win against England.

❛The women sit, getting colder and colder, on a seat getting harder and harder, watching oafs getting muddier and muddier.❜

VIRGINIA GRAHAM.

EARLY DAYS

A HARD GAME

THE FIRST RUGBY CLUB to be formed, Blackheath, came together in 1860. Their rules suggested that the game at the time was a tough one.

Rule 1: "No player may be hacked and held at the same time; hacking above the knee or from behind is unfair. No player can be held or hacked unless he has the ball in his hands. Although it is lawful to hold a player in the scrummage, this does not include attempts to throttle or strangle, which are totally opposed to the principles of the game."

PASSPORTS, PLEASE

THE AMERICAN TEAM for the Olympic Games in 1924 played a series of warm-up matches in England before catching the ferry for France. On arrival at Boulogne, however, the Americans were denied entry because the French Olympic Committee had not forwarded their visas to the port. After a rough crossing, the Americans were understandably not keen on reembarking, and a major fight broke out between rugby players and Gendarmes as the tourists rushed the customs area and broke through. Fortunately an American consular official was able to calm things and gain entry for the squad.

EARLY RISERS

WESTERN SAMOA played their first international fixture in 1924, but requested an early kick-off time of 7am. The reason being that the Western Samoan players had to go to work after the game.

MIND YOUR LANGUAGE

THE ENGLAND VERSUS WALES encounter at Twickenham in January 1927 was the first team game in Britain to be broadcast with radio commentary. The man behind the microphone was Captain HBT Wakelam, and the only advice he was given by his BBC bosses about this brave new world of communicating to the masses came in the form of a note stuck in front of his commentary position at eye level. It said: "Don't Swear!"

FOUR DEFEATS AND ONE LOST

THE FIRST EVER TOUR BY A BRITISH ISLES TEAM TO AUSTRALIA AND NEW ZEALAND took place in 1888. The touring party came back with a creditable record, unbeaten in Australia with 14 out of 16 matches won, and 13 wins and just two defeats in New Zealand. Tragically, though, team captain RL Seddon was drowned during the Australian leg of the tour.

"League is much, much more physical than Union, and that's before anyone started breaking the rules."
ADRIAN HADLEY

‘But Mister, don't you think we're too young to play for Scotland?’

'Rugby may have many problems, but the gravest is undoubtedly that of the persistence of summer.'
CHRIS LAIDLAW.

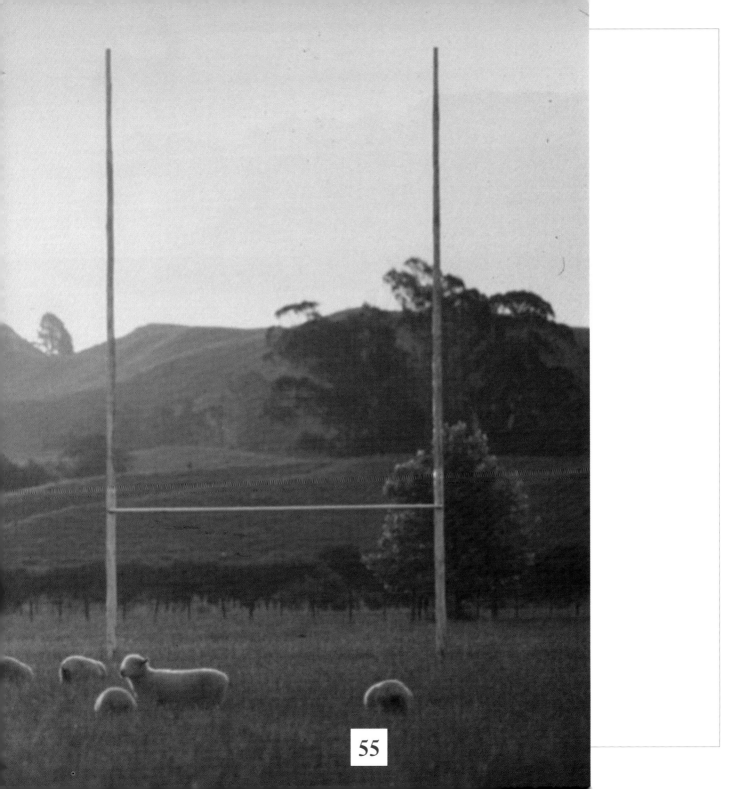

**‘ Forwards are gnarled
and scarred creatures who
have a propensity for
running into and bleeding
all over each other. ’**
PETER FITZSIMMONS

OVERCROWDING

THE RUGBY UNION was formed in 1871, and with it came a full set of laws for the game - which included one which allowed 20 players per side.

THAT'S ALL FOUKES

A MATCH BETWEEN ENGLAND AND IRELAND in 1896 saw the English winger Foukes charge across the try line under the posts, but unfortunately fail to stop in time before crossing the dead ball line. Ireland won 10-4.

LAST RESORT

HAVING USED UP his allotted annual leave from work, Irish player John Macauley took the rather drastic action of getting married in order to get time off to play in an 1887 international match against England.

I BEG YOUR PARDON?

WELSH INTERNATIONAL BOBBY BRICE let fly a stream of invective at the Scottish referee in the 1904 game between Wales and Ireland. Brice thought he would be safe, shouting his abuse in Welsh, but a spectator translated Brice's comments and passed the interpretation to the referee. Brice received a nine month ban.

GOLDEN BOY

ERIC LIDDELL won the 400m gold medal in the 1924 Olympic Games (it was featured in Chariots of Fire), but he also won seven caps for Scotland, and scored four tries.

VERY EARLY BATH

FORMER DERBYSHIRE CRICKETER turned Wilmslow flanker Ewan McCray managed the distinction of being sent off just 30 seconds after the start of a league match against Netherhall.

ACKFORD FELLED BY SCHOOLBOY

ENGLAND BEAT ARGENTINA 51-0 at Twickenham in 1990, but the game will more likely be remembered for the punch which rendered England's giant lock forward unconscious. It was delivered by 18-year-old prop Federico Mendez, and Ackford fell like a tree cut in its prime. Mendez, not surprisingly, was sent off.

FIRST OFF

IRELAND'S WILLIE DUGGAN AND WALES' GEOFF WHEEL earned the distinction of being the first players to be sent off during a Five Nations game. The pair were sent off for exchanging blows in the 1977 clash between the two countries.

RODBER'S WORST

TIM RODBER managed to get himself sent off in an England tour match in 1994 against Eastern Province of South Africa. And to make matters worse he was the captain for that game. It was a violent game, one which saw England's Jon Callard viciously stamped in the face. Rodber said afterwards of his uppercuts which floored opposite number Tremain: "I don't advocate what I did. But someone had to do something. If I had seen Callard's face, I think I would have led the team off the field."

WHY ME?

‘ And while one hand holds the ball, the other hand does THIS! ’

A 30-MAN BRAWL marred the opening game of Argentina's 1995 tour to Australia. The mighty punch-up against ACT ended with Diego Cuesta-Silva, the Argentinian centre, being the one man sent off - about which he had every right to feel aggrieved.

‘Brian Moore shouldn't be allowed to play against women.’

DETENTION TIME

WARWICKSHIRE CLUB SIDE BEDWORTH were forced through an unusual disciplinary procedure after notching up five sendings off. The Midlands Division 2 club were requested to cancel their fixtures for the following weekend and play an in-house game under the dutiful of eye of senior Warwickshire officials. As Bedworth's Keith Brown said: "It was a case of going back to school."

WHAT'S ON TV?

PETER CLOHESSY of Ireland has good reason not to renew his television licence. Playing against France in 1996, the Irish prop was spotted on TV stamping on Olivier Roumat. Clohessey's trial by television resulted in a six month ban. In the 1996 Five Nations, French centre Richard Dourthe was suspended after he was spotted kicking England's Ben Clarke. The crime was not detected until spotted by the BBC the day after the match.

The game's over, and ye bloody will swap shirts.

TIME ON HIS HANDS

IN FEBRUARY 1995, Gloucester forward Simon Devereaux threw a punch at Rosslyn Park's Jamie Cowie. It hit the mark and broke Cowie's jaw. Devereaux had time to regret his action, he was prosecuted for GBH and served four and a half months in Wandsworth Prison.

A GENUINE EARLY BATH

A 1921 GAME between East Midlands and the Barbarians played at Northampton's Franklins Gardens was found to have been stopped 14 minutes short of full-time. The players were brought out of the baths to play out the remaining time.

RULES AND REFS

THE POWER OF TELEVISION

DURING A 1982 MATCH between Mid West and a touring England team, the referee blew for the game to halt just as England had been relentlessly driving towards the opposition goal line. No apparent infringement had taken place on the pitch, so the whistle came as a surprise. The ref then explained that he was merely following instructions to stop the game as the local television station had just gone to a commercial break.

BRAIN STRAIN

WIGAN CAPTAIN SHAUN EDWARDS intimated that his team may only have partial knowledge of the rules of rugby union prior to Wigan's union debut against Bath. "You have to have six O-levels to understand them all."

THANKS REF

COMPETING in the Hong Kong Carlsberg 10s tournament which precedes the rather bigger 7s event, Wolverhampton Polytechnic Old Boys, a team of ex-Poly players who average about one game a season, found themselves through to the quarter final stages, where they met more than their match in the form of Tokyo Gaijin - a team of expatriates based in Japan, and red hot favourites to win that particular competition.

Wolves were completely overrun, and when they finally did put pressure on the Tokyo line, the Irish referee, obviously taking pity on the former students, awarded them a penalty try, thus ensuring Wolverhampton at least registered on the scoreboard. Wolves' fly-half John Corr then offered the referee the opportunity to take the conversion, which he duly drop kicked straight through the posts. He finished the game as Wolves' only scorer on the day.

THOU SHALT NOT GRAB MORE THAN ONE BALL

FOR THE 1997 SEASON, referees in the Super 12s tournament played in the southern hemisphere have agreed to outlaw the act of grabbing a players' testicles. A player found breaking the rule will be sent off and face a two year ban. Top Australian referee Peter Marshall commented: "It is hard to detect. It depends on how much water is coming out of a player's eyes."

DODGY REF

RUGBY PLAYERS are well known for questioning the decisions of a referee, usually in the bar afterwards. But two Irish players made their feelings clear during a match against Wales in 1882. They walked off in protest at the somewhat questionable decisions of referee Richard Mullock, who also happened to be secretary of the Welsh Rugby Union.

'You've got to get your first tackle in early - even if it's late.'

RAY GRAVELL.

"I think you enjoy the game more if you don't know the rules. Anyway, you're on the same wavelength as referees."

JONATHAN DAVIES

"There is still a lot of flatulence emanating from the RFU and in our view a professional game has to be administered by professionals."

EPRUC CHIEF EXECUTIVE KIM DESHAYES.

The dramatic moment during the 1997 Wales v Ireland match at Cardiff Arms Park when referee J.M. Steveson announced his controversial decision to henceforth live his life as a woman.

"No leadership, no ideas. Not even enough imagination to thump someone in the lineout when the ref wasn't looking."

JPR WILLIAMS LAMENTS ANOTHER WELSH DEFEAT.

Get up Ben.
This is no time
for your
Norman Wisdom
impressions.

'Bloody Lomu.'

FOR ANORAKS
(RUGBY RECORDS)

LEAKY DEFENCE

IRELAND'S RECORD OF CONCEDING 141 POINTS in the Five Nations tournament of 1997 set a new landmark in the history of the event. The previous record holders, the 1992 Irish side, lost all four games but conceded 25 fewer points. The 1997 side at least beat Wales but their record of 18 tries conceded in four games was two worse than 1992.

GUSCOTT'S FINEST

JEREMY GUSCOTT'S DEBUT against Romania in Bucharest in 1989 was an explosive one for England's latest find at centre. He scored three tries in a 58-3 win.

THE MIGHTY ALL BLACKS

THE ALL BLACKS hold the record for the most consecutive international victories: - 17 between 1965 and 1969. And between 1987 and 1990 they went 23 internationals without defeat.

FRANCE'S BLEAK YEARS

THE YEARS BETWEEN 1910 AND 1913 were not happy ones for the French international team. France's record defeats against each of the Home Nations in the Five Nations Championship occurred in these years. In 1910 against Wales, 1911 against England, 1912 against Scotland and 1913 against Ireland.

YOUNG WILL

WHEN WILL CARLING WAS APPOINTED ENGLAND CAPTAIN in 1988, he was aged just 22, the youngest England captain for 57 years.

HOME TIME

PRIOR TO 1997, France had never managed to clinch the Grand Slam in front of a home crowd. Previous Grand Slams for France have been sealed in Ireland (twice), at Twickenham and at Cardiff Arms Park.

PUT TO THE SWORD

THE MATCH BETWEEN JAPAN AND NEW ZEALAND in the 1995 World Cup set a host of new rugby records, most of which the Japanese will want to forget. The final score of 145-17 in favour of the All Blacks was the biggest winning margin in an official match between international board countries. New Zealand's 145 is also the highest score attained in an international, and it contained the most tries, 21, and the most conversions, 20.

IRELAND'S STRUGGLE

IRELAND have not won the Five Nations Grand Slam since 1948, which is the worst record of all the countries competing.

INDIVIDUAL CAP RECORDS

Most capped player: Philippe Sella (France) 111 caps (1982-1995)

Most caps in a position:

Full back: Serge Blanco 81 out of 93 caps

Wing: Rory Underwood 91

Centre: Sella 104

Fly Half: Rob Andrew 74

Scrum Half: Gareth Edwards 63

Prop: Phil Orr (Ire) 59

Hooker: Sean Fitzpatrick 73

Lock: Willie John McBride (Ire) 80

Flanker: John Slattery (Ire) 65 and Peter Winterbottom 65

No. 8: Dean Richards 53

GAVIN HASTINGS of Scotland is the British Lions' most prolific scorer, notching 66 points in his six test appearances. Tony O'Reilly of Ireland, now the top man with Heinz, holds the record for most test tries by a Lion, with six from 10 appearances between 1955 and 1959.

THE ALL BLACKS longest losing sequence of matches is just six, in 1949. Wales actually have managed to outdo the All Blacks here, the longest Welsh losing sequence is five matches, which has happened twice. In 1989/90 and 1994/5.

ENGLAND FLY HALF PAUL GRAYSON equalled Grant Fox's record of reaching 100 international points in his sixth game - against Scotland in 1997.

IRELAND HAVE NOT BEATEN FRANCE FOR 11 YEARS.

NEIL JENKINS became the first Welshman to notch up 500 points in test matches during the 1997 victory over Scotland. He is the fifth player in rugby history to do so.

JONAH LOMU became the youngest ever All Black when picked at the age of 19 to play against France. However, he was dropped after one game because of his defensive frailties.

VAÍAIGA TUIGAMALA has the distinction of being the first player to score a five point try in an international match.

> "The most misleading campaign of 1991: England's rugby World Cup squad, who promoted a scheme called "Run With The Ball". Not, unfortunately, among themselves."
> TIME OUT

Let's see if Danny Baker can get the stains out of these.

DAVID CAMPESE is the highest international try scorer of all time.

MOST CAPPED BRITISH LION is Willie John McBride of Ireland, who represented the Lions on 17 occasions between 1962 and 1974. This included a run of 15 consecutive test appearances in a Lions jersey.

THE FIRST FULLY REPRESENTATIVE BRITISH ISLES TOUR, with the four Home Unions actually co-operating with each other, was to South Africa in 1910. The Test series was lost 2-1.

GRANT FOX is the fastest player to 200 international points, taking just 13 games to hit the landmark.

> "A forward's usefulness to his side varies as to the square of his distance from the ball."
> CLARRIE GIBBONS

> "Tony Ward is the most important rugby player in Ireland. His legs are far more important to his country than even those of Marlene Dietrich were to the film industry. A little hairier, maybe, but a pair of absolute winners."
> MIKE GIBSON

> "We are not ashamed to admit that we could not afford to pay players or officials, nor indeed would we want to."
> PHIL MITCHELL, CHAIRMAN OF HARTLEPOOL ROVERS

Halitosis..

Ireland's
Jonathan Bell's
armpits drive his
teammates off
the pitch..

The Western Samoans are brought to their knees by their on double-armpit assault on England..

French players are overcome by Jason Leonard's personal mustard gas..

IN TRAINING

TIMES HAVE CHANGED when it comes to preparing for a big game- the advent of professionalism has seen to that. It was different in the old days, as Arthur Harding, London Welsh Captain, told The Sportsman in an interview given in 1901: "I indulge in walking as much as possible; it is a fine exercise. I am a smoker, but I knock off the weed a week or so before an international match, and add to my walking a little running."

BRICKING IT

THE ALL BLACKS BECAME THE ALL BRICKS in 1980 when coach Eric Watson introduced a new training exercise to help rid the players of their propensity to drop passes. Instead of a ball, the players trained with a brick.

BREAD OF HEAVEN

IN 1991, as England prepared to break their Cardiff hoodoo, England manager Geoff Cooke employed some interesting psychological preparations. At a training session prior to the game, the England squad ran on to the pitch to the strains of the Welsh national anthem, which was played again as the team journeyed to Cardiff, and several more times in the build up to the match. It worked, England won 25-6.

FORWARDS CAUGHT SHORT

TRAINING in the England squads' first session of the 1986/7 season was enlivened by the presence of British Olympic shot-putter Judy Oakes. She challenged the English forwards to a bench press competition, and wiped the floor with the lot of them.

HIS OWN MAN

DEAN RICHARDS has a reputation of doing things his own way, and he was one of the England squad who never got to grips with manager Geoff Cooke's psychological training. In fact, Cooke's famous motivational tape, supplied to all players, did not stay long in Deano's possession. He deposited it in the bin.

‘Beaumont was like a St Bernard, a loveable, bulky, gentle old thing possessing great strength under the graceful floppy exterior, someone who would always come to your rescue.’
CLEM THOMAS.

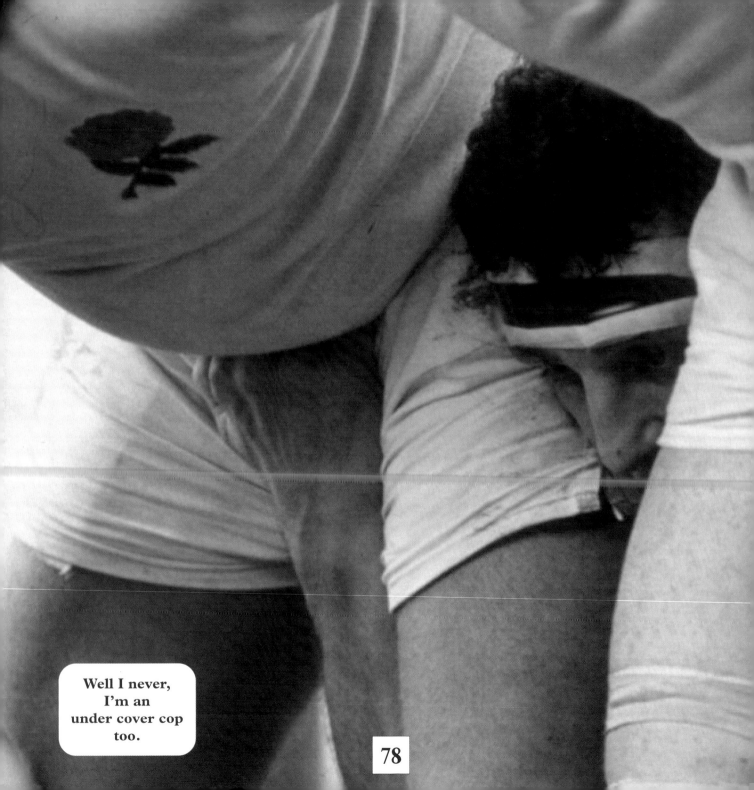

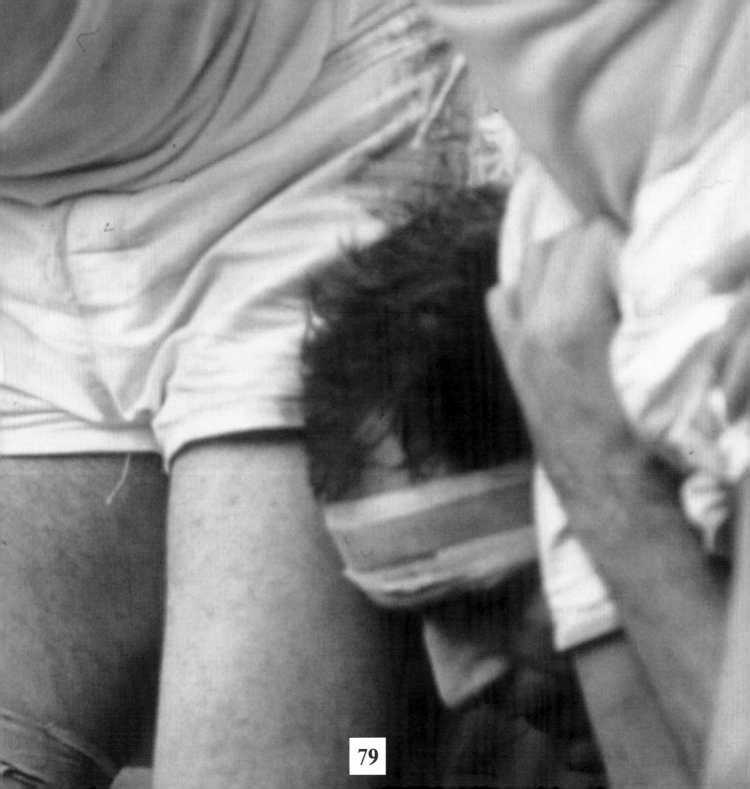

79

E A C H   T O   T H E I R   O W N

SO WHAT DO INTERNATIONAL RUGBY PLAYERS DO in their spare time now that professionalism is upon us? While golf and the cinema feature highly for filling free time, there are some more bizarre hobbies. Will Carling for example, enjoys the tranquillity of painting. Ireland's Michael Bradley gets to grips with landscape gardening and Scotland's Damian Cronin fancies himself as a bit of an antiques expert. But there must be something about playing in the front row. Irish prop Peter Clohessy likes water skiing, Welsh prop Mike Griffiths goes mountain biking, and England hooker Grahame Dawe lists his non-rugby pursuits as bell ringing and sheep shearing!

"I thought I would have a quiet pint, followed by about 17 noisy ones."

G A R E T H ' C O O C H Y '
C H I L C O T T O N H I S
R E T I R E M E N T D A Y P L A N S .

> **'To any sport, amusement or pastime, indoor or outdoor, bar rugby football, bad weather simply spells no gate and empty benches.'**
> SOUTH WALES REPORTER

ACE CAMPO

THE MERCURIAL RUGBY TALENTS of David Campese are legend, but he's no mean golfer, either. To such an extent that he can boast winning the 1981 ACT Schools Championship in Australia.

WILL'S RETREAT

WHAT WOULD WILL CARLING like to be marooned on a desert island with? He told Radio 4's Desert Island Discs that a copy of The Hobbit to read, Louis Armstrong's What A Wonderful World to listen to and flotation tank to lie in would suit him just fine.

NO SALE FOR HORAN

AUSTRALIAN CENTRE TIM HORAN appeared on Sale of the Century but managed to answer only one question correctly.

HANGOVER CURE

SCOTLAND CENTRE IAN JARDINE evidently enjoys his game and the apres-rugby. After a rather heavy session in the bar after a Scotland B game, Jardine manged to drink his wife's contact lenses which she had left beside the bed.

LET HIM EAT CAKE

MICKEY SKINNER, after winning only his second England cap, nearly caused an international incident with Wales after the 1988 Five Nations match. Skinner decided to play waiter with one of the large cream cakes, and standing behind Welsh flanker Rowland Phillips, asked "would sir like some cake?" Phillips did not turn round but indicated he would like some, whereupon Skinner shoved the lot in Phillips' face.

'Are you married?'

Not So Smart

COLIN SMART, England prop, has a place in rugby folklore for one of his post match exploits. After the 1982 game against France in Paris, Smart and lock forward Maurice Colclough engaged in a drinking duel. Colclough, though, had an ace up his sleeve. Each player at the post match dinner was presented with a bottle of aftershave. Colclough surreptitiously emptied his and refilled it with tap water. During the dinner, he picked up the bottle of now harmless "aftershave", turned to Smart, and drank it down in one. Smart, sensing a challenge but not realising the ruse, picked up his bottle of genuine aftershave, and drank it down with equal speed. He was able to laugh off the incident after having his stomach pumped at hospital.

Scot's Banker

DURING THE POST MATCH DINNER for the 1986 match between Scotland and France, president of the Scottish Rugby Union George Burrell was able to witness a potentially catastrophic incident first hand. Burrell was entertaining a senior official from the Royal Bank of Scotland, whom he was trying to entice into a sponsorship deal for the national team. As Burrell made his speech to the assembled players and officials, a tomato was launched from the players' table, and unerringly hit the Bank representative square on the chest, exploding on impact.

At the next squad session, Burrell berated the players saying: "We're in the midst of delicate negotiations and you lot have got us off to a fine ******* start!" He never discovered the identity of the marksman, though.

What Flavour?

GAVIN HASTINGS witnessed one of the more amazing drinking games when on tour in Singapore. The Sun Solarians were, by all accounts, a big drinking team, and one of their number had his own special party trick. He drank six pints of milk - first two normal, then two chocolate milks and finally two strawberry milks. He then regurgitated the milks to order. If someone wanted strawberry, he would vomit the strawberry milk. Or the chocolate if so requested. As Hastings said: "It was an incredible sight."

Are You Starting Something?

ON THE 1974 LIONS TOUR to South Africa, some hotel high jinks occurred and a room was trashed. The manager wanted to call the police. Lions captain Willie John McBride, a strict disciplinarian, said that the culprits would be severely reprimanded and all damages paid for. The manager still wanted to call the police. McBride reiterated that costs would be met and punishments handed out. Still the manager wanted to call the police. Flanked by some of the Lions' forwards, who were not small, McBride drew himself up and towered over the manger saying: "And tell me Mr Manager. How many of these 'police' do you have?"

"Rembrandt created masterpieces with a brush and paint, Shakespeare expressed himself using a quill and paper, while Mozart turned individual musical instruments into a symphony of wondrous melodic sound. All David Campese needed was a football and field of grass."
GREG CAMPBELL IN RW ON CAMPESE:

"Lomu is a martian,
an extra-terrestrial."

GEORGE COSTE,
ITALIAN COACH

'Oh Gawd.'

"I'd rather play for
Gloucester for 10p than go
to Newcastle for £85,000."

PHIL GREENING
OF GLOUCESTER.

❝I fancy him,
so I'm gonna
have him.❞

LEAGUE WINS

1996 SAW THE ADVENT OF THE RUGBY CHALLENGE MATCH, a series of two games between rugby union champions Bath and rugby league champions Wigan. In the first match, played to league rules, Wigan ran out winners 82-6. Bath won the union encounter 44-19, but Wigan rubbed salt in the wounds of union fans by winning the Middlesex 7s tournament with ease.

> **"The International Board jumped off the high board not knowing whether there was any water in the pool below."**
> GARETH EDWARDS ON PROFESSIONALISM

IS THAT ADVERTISING?

ON TOUR IN JAPAN in the 1970s, the Scottish team had been given T-shirts as a gift by a local bus company, which of course featured the company's logo. The Scottish Rugby Union, nervous of accusations of professionalism, decreed that the players could wear the shirts, but only if they were turned inside out.

STRIKE THREAT

IN 1991, the French players threatened to go on strike just days before the World Cup was due to kick off because they wanted cash incentives to play.

WHICH BALL SHALL WE USE?

THE NEW ERA OF PROFESSIONALISM can throw up the odd unexpected problem. For example, the Wasps ground sharing scheme with football club QPR has led to some interesting ticketing for matches such as: Queens Park Rangers to play Bath at home. It would be an interesting confrontation.

WINDY WILL

WILL CARLING managed to put the cat among the pigeons when he ventured to suggest that the Rugby Football Union was run by 57 old farts. Fair enough if it was a whispered aside in the pub, but the England captain made his statement on national television, and was sacked in the fall-out. Public outcry and player power saw him reinstated to his rightful position.

> **"There are many evils in the world, but two of the worst are money and greed."**
> WILLIE JOHN MCBRIDE ON PROFESSIONALISM

EYES ON THE ROAD

WELSH FLANKER EMYR LEWIS was flying down the flank in support of his backs when playing for Cardiff against Northampton. Unfortunately, Lewis did not keep his eyes on the road in front, tripped over and twisted his ankle.

WHO PUT THAT THERE?

MICHAEL LYNAGH OF AUSTRALIA, once manged to run straight into the posts while watching the ball in attempting to catch an up and under.

SORRY REF

SCOTTISH HOOKER KENNY MILNE comes from a distinguished rugby family, both his brothers have also represented Scotland, but neither can lay claim to anything like one of Kenny's less momentous occasions. As the Heriots and Jed Forest front rows readied themselves for a set-to, Milne threw a punch, missed his target and instead flattened the referee.

"I don't know about us not having a Plan B when things went wrong, we looked like we didn't have a Plan A."

GEOFF COOKE AFTER ENGLAND'S DEFEAT AGAINST THE ALL BLACKS IN THE 1995 WORLD CUP.

"We tried to handle the ball in the wrong places, and I blame the media for that."

JACK ROWELL

"The French selectors never do anything by halves; for the first international of the season against Ireland they dropped half the three quarter line."

NIGEL STARMER-SMITH

❛The rugby player during the course of a game is living life at its most intoxicating.❜

ROWE HARDING

94

I'm a cert for Playgirl, me.

ROSE'S BONUS

IF ENGLAND HIT A NADIR IN THE 1980S it came at Cardiff in 1987, a place where England hadn't won since 1963. Two fired up sets of forwards sparked a brawl which saw English lock Wade Dooley break Phil Davies' cheekbone with a haymaker and after the match England's Dooley, Chilcott, Dawe and captain Richard Hill were all suspended by the RFU.

The Welsh crowd threw coins at England full back Marcus Rose, who collected £3.50, gave it to the referee and asked him to hold onto it until afterwards so Rose could spend it in the bar.

"Look what these bastards have done to Wales. They've taken our coal, our water, our steel. They buy our houses and they only live in them for a fortnight a year. What have they given us? Absolutely nothing. We've been exploited, raped, controlled and punished by the English - and that's who you are playing this afternoon."

A PHIL BENNETT TEAM PEP TALK.

❛ Sport is an unfailing cause of ill will.❜

GEORGE ORWELL

"I used to enjoy playing sevens, although you have to be something of a masochist to take that view. Sevens is a form of physical torture that has to be experienced to be believed."

BILL McLAREN

"If I had been a winger, I might have been daydreaming and thinking about how to keep my kit clean for next week."

BILL BEAUMONT

"Everyone knows that there is a loose wire between Campo's brain and his mouth."

BOB DWYER

❛Sports do not build character. They reveal it.❜

HEYWOOD BROWN

LIFE'S A RIOT

IN THE 1924 OLYMPIC FINAL, the USA played France in a hostile and partisan atmosphere. When French player Mercel Frederic Lubin punched the American centre Dick Hayland in the face, Welsh referee Sam Freethy had no choice but to send Lubin off, thus reducing the French team to 13 (they had already lost one player through injury). US captain Babe Slater saw the mood of the crowd degenerate and asked the referee to reconsider his decision. Freethy refused at first, then told Slater to fetch the Frenchman back if he wanted him. Lubin was reluctant to return, so Slater walked after him, picked him up, and carried him back to his position on the field.

The eventual American victory was greeted by rioting in the crowds.

A TALE OF TWO CODES

IS THERE A GAP between the fitness levels of players of rugby league and rugby union? Former coach of Wigan, Graham Lowe seems to think so. "I'm 49, I've had a brain haemorrhage and a triple bypass and I could still go out and play a reasonable game of rugby union. But I wouldn't last 30 seconds in rugby league."

FARES PLEASE

FRENCH PROP Gerard Cholley holds the reputation, among strong competition, of being one of the hardest men to put on the famous blue jersey. During a 1977 game against Scotland, Cholley laid Scotland's No.8 Don McDonald low with one mighty punch, and also inflicted severe damage on others. Such was the carnage inflicted by the former French paratrooper that England's Mike Burton later wrote that Cholley's demolition of the Scottish pack that day was done in the manner of "a bus conductor proceeding up the aisle taking fares."

HESLOP AMBUSHED

THE 1991 WORLD CUP ENCOUNTER BETWEEN ENGLAND AND FRANCE was also the venue for a fearsome assault on England winger Nigel Heslop. Heslop ran into a barrage of punches from French flanker Eric Champ and full back Serge Blanco. Heslop had to leave the pitch.

How To Earn Respect

WHEN TWO AMBULANCEMEN ran on to the pitch to try to get groggy French scrum half Pierre Danos onto a stretcher during a 1958 match between Northern Transvaal and France, there seemed to be a breakdown in communications. Danos did not want to leave the pitch, and to emphasise the point, his prop forward, Alfred Rocques treated one of the stretcher bearers to a huge uppercut, which laid him prostrate. As they prepared the stretcher for the medic, he jumped to his feet, bowed to Rocques, shouted "Vive La France" and left the pitch.

Lost In Translation

AFTER A TOUGH AND VIOLENT TOUR OF ARGENTINA, Scotland's Jim Telfer did not mince his words at the final dinner. "If you wish to be accepted internationally," he told the Argentine squad and officials, "you must cut out the dirty play. In all my time in the game I have never come up against an opposition so set on intimidatory tactics."

However, his speech of a few minutes only took a matter of seconds for the interpreter to translate. When Telfer asked what he had said, he was told: "I thought it best just to use that bit about what a beautiful country this is. I did not want to risk an international incident."

"The South Africans train for some 26 hours a week and the Pumas may train for about eight hours if they can make it."

ARGENTINA PUMAS CAPTAIN LISANDRO ARBIZU ON THE WIDENING GAP IN MODERN RUGBY.

A Hard Game

ALL BLACK LEGEND WAYNE SHELFORD had good reason to remember New Zealand's 1986 defeat at the hands of France in Nantes. The French set about the All Blacks like men possessed, indeed Shelford later said he thought they must have been on drugs, and the levels of violence were high. Shelford himself finished the match with concussion, three teeth knocked out, and his right testicle ripped out of his scrotum.

'There's no doubt about it, he's a big bastard.'
GAVIN HASTINGS

"To me rugby is an opportunity to show how creative you can be and I know what can be done if you decide to have a go. I can accept losing if you've at least had a go. But to lose and be boring in the process is something that can only be detrimental to rugby. Those who can't break the defence by running the ball or setting up their backline should not be on the field."

CAMPO

Dean Richards is nicknamed Warren, as in 'warren ugly bastard'.

JASON LEONARD.

IF YOU ENJOYED THIS BOOK,
WHAT ABOUT THESE!

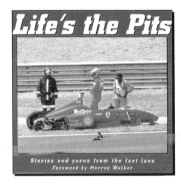

All these books are available at your local book shop or can be ordered direct from the publisher.
Just list the titles you require and give your name address, including post code.
Prices and availability are subject to change without notice.

Please send to Chameleon Cash Sales, 106 Great Russell Street London WCIB 3LJ, a cheque or
postal order for £7.99 and add the following for postage and packaging:

UK - £1.00 For the first book. 50p for the second and 30p for the third for each additional book
up to a maximum of £3.00.
OVERSEAS -(including Eire) £2.00 For the first book and £1.00 for the second and 50p for
each additional book up to a maximum of £3.00.